CAMBRIDGE
UNIVERSITY PRESS

CAMBRIDGE ENGLISH
Language Assessment
Part of the University of Cambridge

W0099548

Cambridge English

Movers 8

Student's Book

CAMBRIDGE
UNIVERSITY PRESS

University Printing House, Cambridge CB2 8BS, United Kingdom

Cambridge University Press is part of the University of Cambridge.

It furthers the University's mission by disseminating knowledge in the pursuit of education, learning and research at the highest international levels of excellence.

www.cambridge.org
Information on this title: www.cambridge.org/9781107613072

© Cambridge University Press 2013

This publication is in copyright. Subject to statutory exception and to the provisions of relevant collective licensing agreements, no reproduction of any part may take place without the written permission of Cambridge University Press.

First published 2013
5th printing 2015

Printed in China by Golden Cup Printing Co. Ltd

A catalogue record for this publication is available from the British Library

ISBN 978-1-107-61307-2 Student's Book
ISBN 978-1-107-69089-9 Answer Booklet
ISBN 978-1-107-61785-8 Audio CD

Cover design by Peter & Jan Simmonett
Produced by Kamae Design, Oxford

Cambridge University Press has no responsibility for the persistence or accuracy of URLs for external or third-party internet websites referred to in this publication, and does not guarantee that any content on such websites is, or will remain, accurate or appropriate. Information regarding prices, travel timetables, and other factual information given in this work is correct at the time of first printing but Cambridge University Press does not guarantee the accuracy of such information thereafter.

Contents

Test 1

Listening

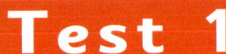

Part 1

– 5 questions –

Listen and draw lines. There is one example.

Sally Anna Paul Vicky

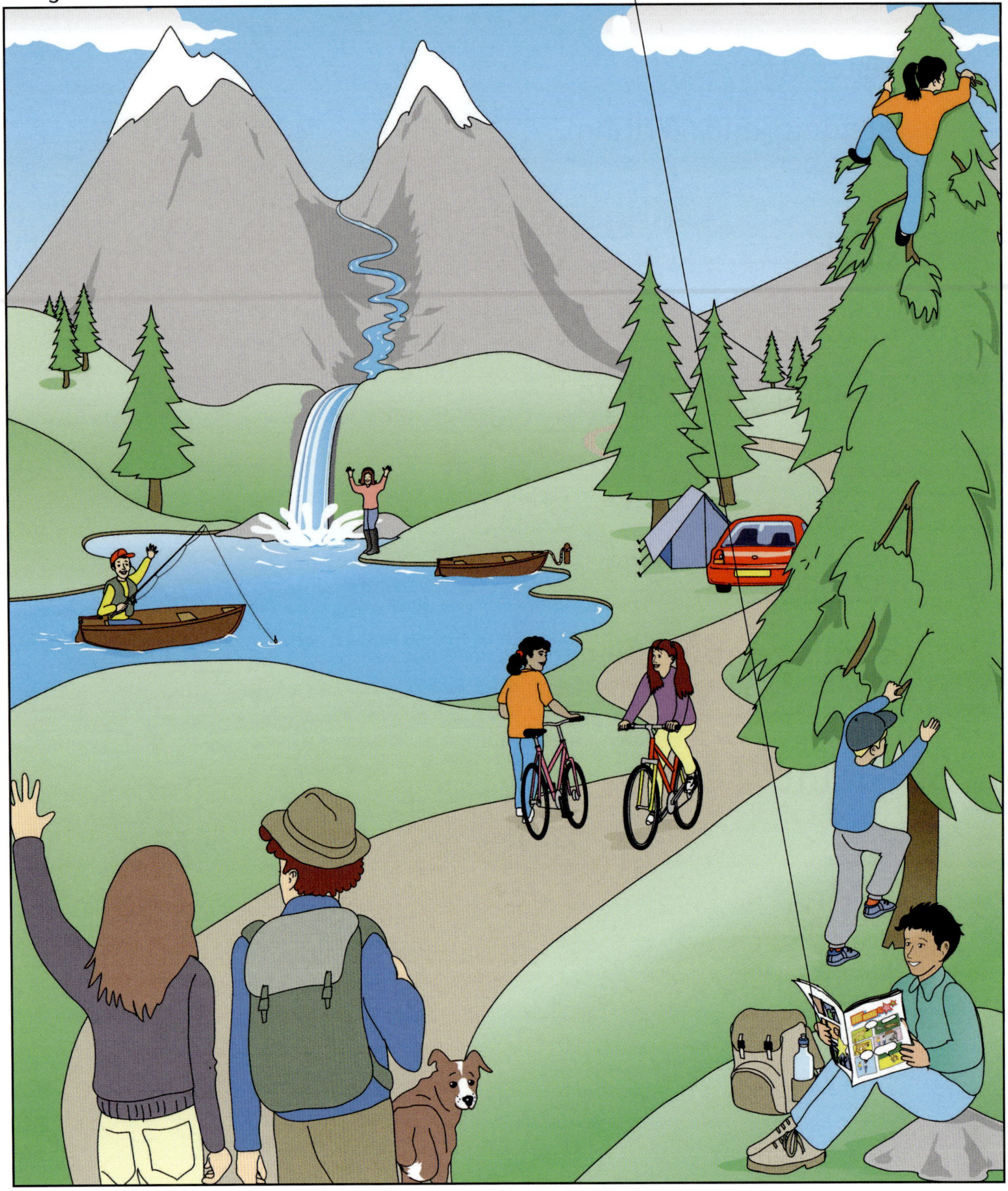

Bill Lucy John

Part 2

– 5 questions –

Listen and write. There is one example.

Things lost in school

	What?	*School bag*
1	Colour?	
2	Where lost?	*in*
3	What was inside?	
4	Child's name?	*Jill*
5	Child's class number?	

Part 3
– 5 questions –

What did Tony do last week?

Listen and draw a line from the day to the correct picture.

There is one example.

Monday

Tuesday

Wednesday

Thursday

Friday

Saturday

Sunday

Part 4
– 5 questions –

Listen and tick (✔) the box. There is one example.

What's Lucy's father doing?

A ☐   B ☐   C ✔

1   Where's the new bird cage?

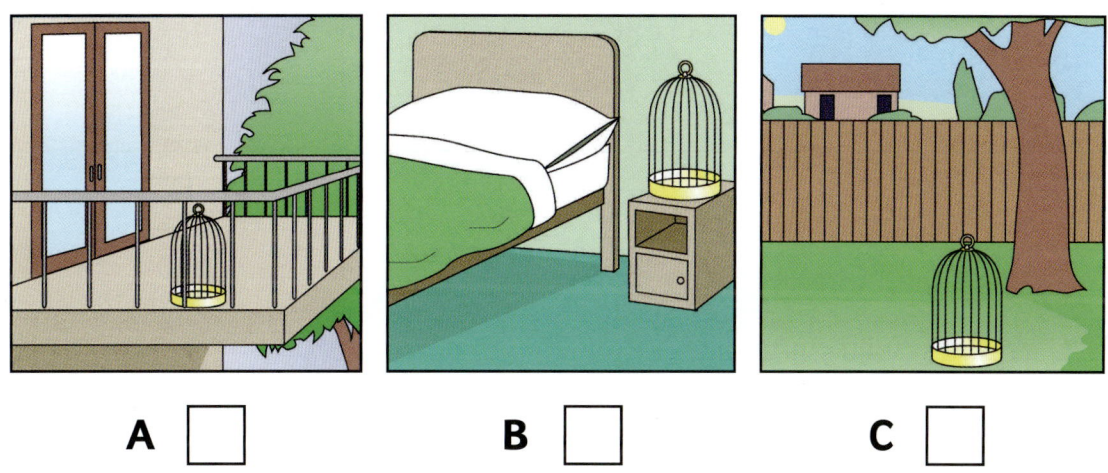

A ☐   B ☐   C ☐

2   How did Peter go to work today?

A ☐   B ☐   C ☐

3   Which is Tom's favourite sport?

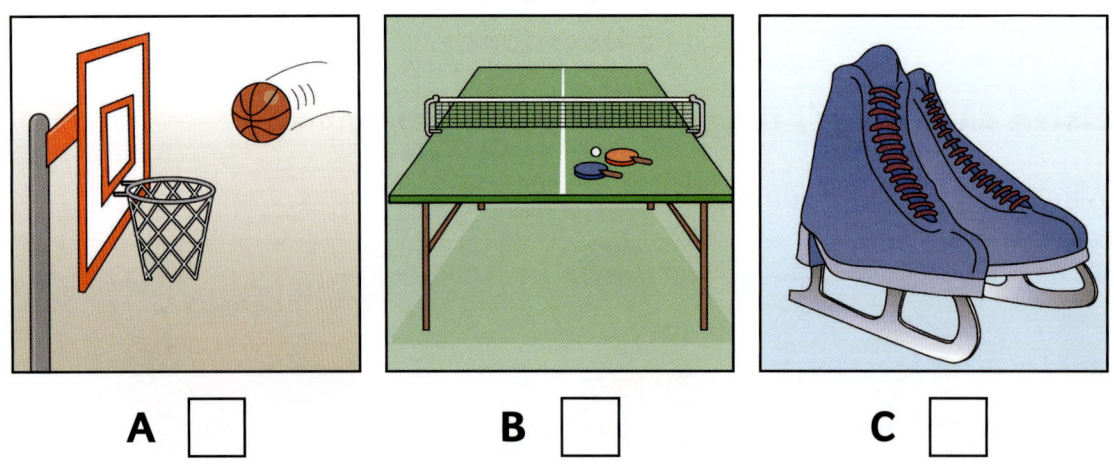

A ☐   B ☐   C ☐

4   What did May buy in the shop today?

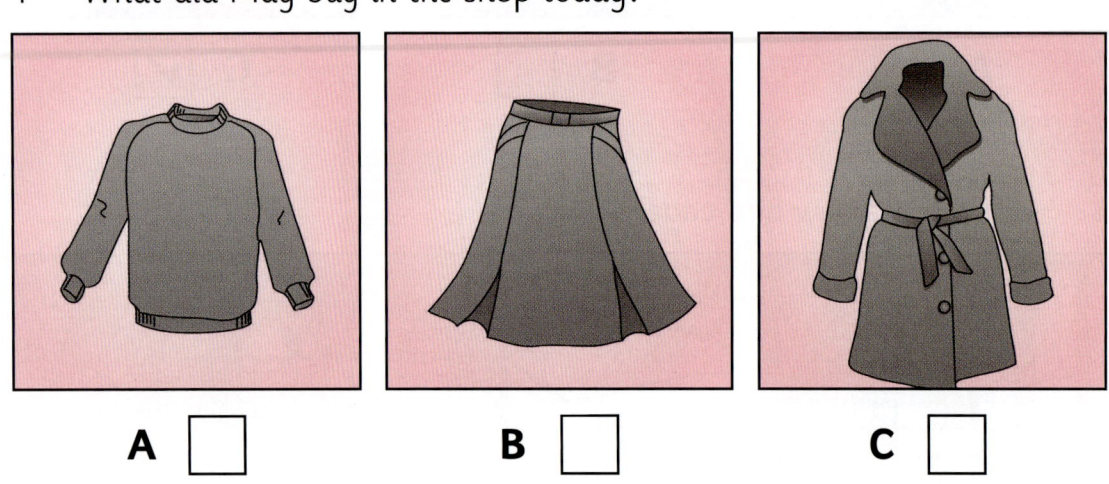

A ☐   B ☐   C ☐

5   Where's Sally's grandma?

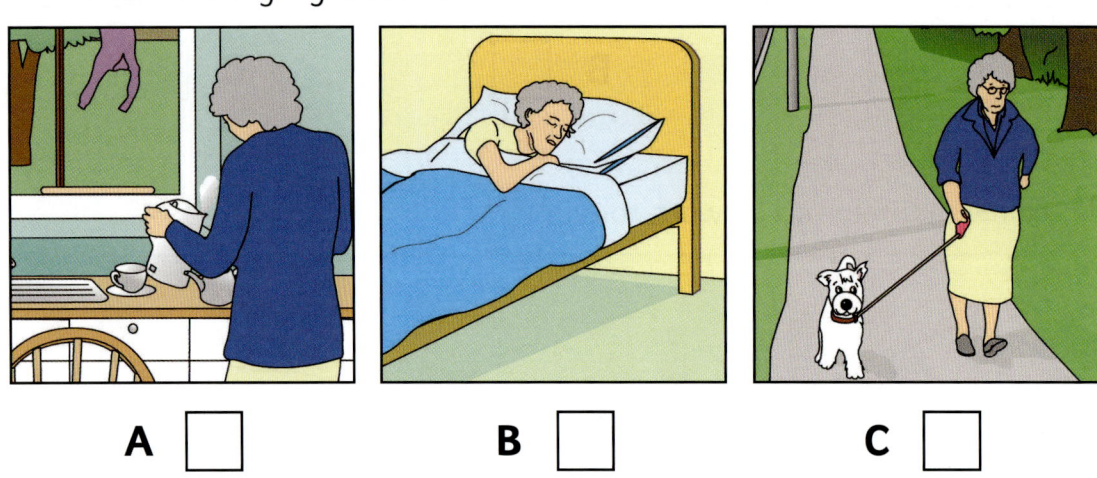

A ☐   B ☐   C ☐

Part 5
– 5 questions –

Listen and colour and write. There is one example.

Reading and Writing

Part 1
– 6 questions –

Look and read. Choose the correct words and write them on the lines. There is one example.

snow

a city

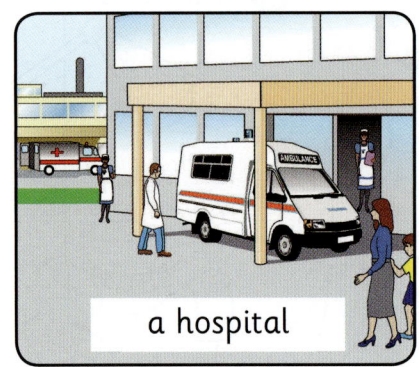
a hospital

fields

leaves

clouds

a jungle

stars

Example

This place is hot and there are lots of different kinds of plants in it.

.... *a jungle* ....

Questions

1   You can only see these at night.

....

2   Farms have these. You see cows or sheep in them sometimes.

....

3   This is a place that has a lot of houses, shops and people in it.

....

4   Children who live in very cold places can play in this.

....

5   These are often grey and give us rain.

....

6   You can see these on most trees.

....

Part 2
– 6 questions –

Look and read. Write yes or no.

Examples

A whale is behind the big rock in the sea. ....*yes*.............

There are five trees on the island. ....*no*.............

Questions

1 A parrot is flying above the boat. ....

2 A girl who has got long hair is
   running in the water. ....

3 There are two glasses of orange juice
   on the towel. ....

4 You can see a toy kangaroo between
   the bag and the ball. ....

5 The woman has a book in her hands
   and is wearing a watch. ....

6 The weather at the beach is cold,
   windy and wet. ....

Part 3
– 6 questions –

Read the text and choose the best answer.

Jim and his uncle are talking about a film.

Example

Jim's uncle:	Did you go and see that new film, Jim?

Jim:	A	Yes, it was!
	B	Yes, I did!
	C	Yes, you are!

Questions

1	**Jim's uncle:**	When did you go?

Jim:	A	Outside the cinema.
	B	We went on the bus.
	C	On Monday afternoon.

2   **Jim's uncle:**   Which cinema did you go to?

   Jim: A   He went there.
            B   The one by the park.
            C   It's a kind of place.

3   **Jim's uncle:**   So, did you enjoy the film?

   Jim: A   It was great.
            B   All right.
            C   I'm fine.

4   **Jim's uncle:**   Who did you go with?

   Jim: A   Mum and Peter.
            B   He often goes.
            C   There they are.

5   **Jim's uncle:**   Were there a lot of people there?

   Jim: A   Yes, here they are.
            B   Yes, she goes a lot.
            C   Yes, there were.

6   **Jim's uncle:**   And what did you do after the film, Jim?

   Jim: A   I'd like to do that.
            B   We had a burger.
            C   You can watch it.

Part 4

– 7 questions –

Read the story. Choose a word from the box. Write the correct word next to numbers 1–6. There is one example.

One day, Mary found a book in the ....*library*.............. . It was about

clowns. She loved the story and she **(1)** .... her grandma

all about it. 'I want to be a clown now!' Mary said.

'Well, come and look at this,' her grandmother answered and

(2) .... to a big, old box. 'Open it, Mary,' she said.

Inside the box, there were lots of clothes. Mary took them out. She put on

the biggest shirt and the longest trousers and a hat with flowers on it.

Then Grandma coloured Mary's nose with red **(3)** ....

She also gave Mary some black shoes and one yellow and one purple

(4) .... to wear.

'Now go and look in the big **(5)** .... in my bedroom,

Mary,' she said.

Mary went up the **(6)** .... to her grandmother's room

and looked at her face and clothes. She laughed and said, 'I AM a

clown now!'

Example

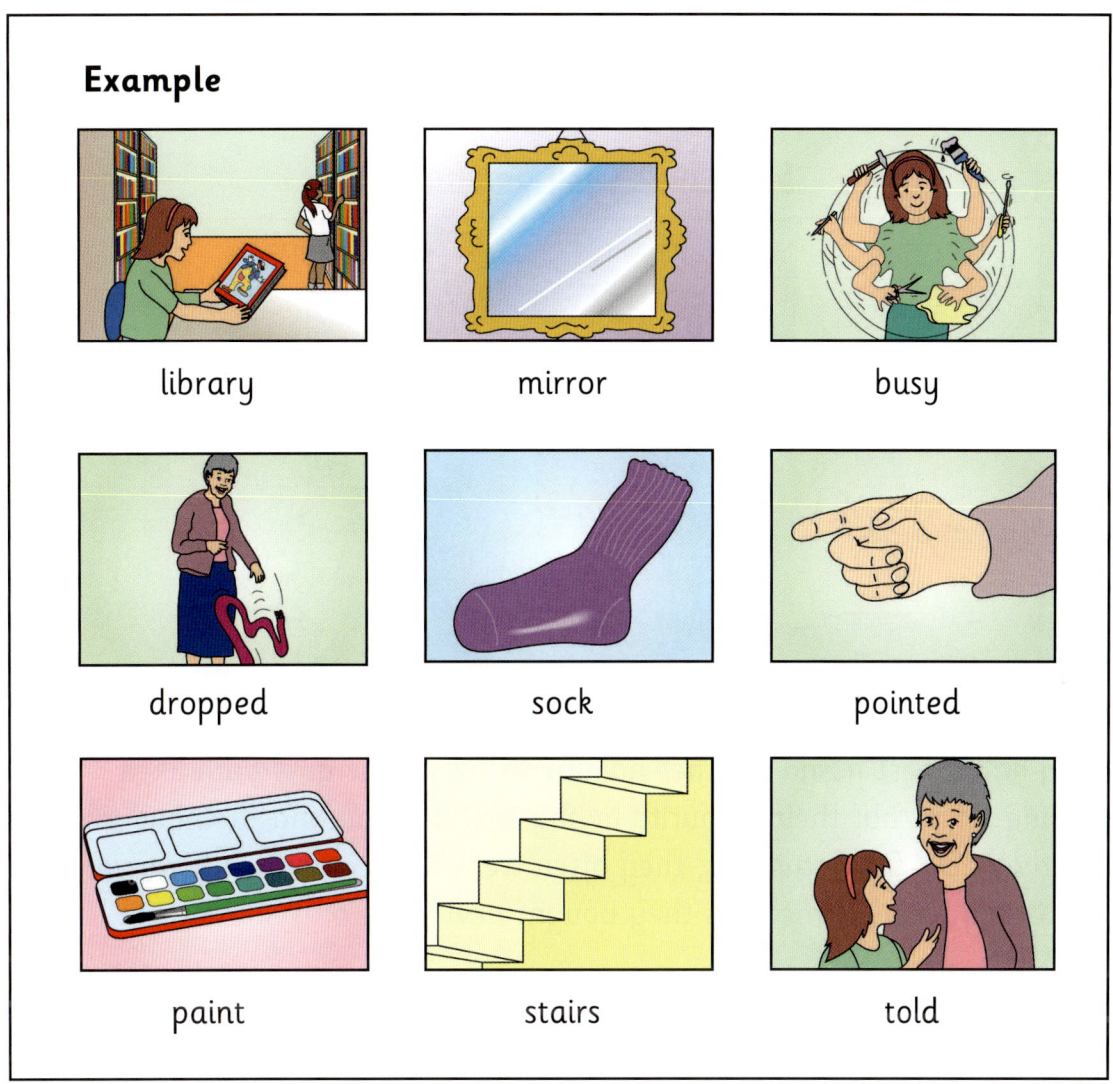

library	mirror	busy
dropped	sock	pointed
paint	stairs	told

(7) Now choose the best name for the story.

Tick one box.

Grandma's book for clowns ☐

Mary and the clown's clothes ☐

A clown comes to school ☐

Part 5
– 10 questions –

Look at the pictures and read the story. Write some words to complete the sentences about the story. You can use 1, 2 or 3 words. There are two examples.

<u>Sally and Lucy go shopping</u>

Sally had a best friend and her name was Lucy. The girls both liked playing tennis but their favourite hobby was dancing and they had lots of great CDs. On Saturdays, they often went to the shops in town with Sally's big sister. Sometimes they bought new jeans or T-shirts there.

Examples

Sally's best friend is called ....Lucy.............. .

The two friends ....liked playing......... tennis.

Questions

1   Sally and Lucy liked .... best.

2   The girls often went shopping on ....

3   .... went to the town with Sally and Lucy.

One morning, Sally said to her dad, 'It's Lucy's party on Sunday. Can I have a new dress to wear for it?'

'Yes!' he said. 'But you never wear dresses, Sally!'

'Well, it's easier to dance in jeans,' she answered. 'But I'd like a dress for the party.'

'There's a market today,' he said. 'We can go and find you a dress there.'

And they did. Sally's dad bought her a beautiful white one.

4   Sally talked to .... about Lucy's party.

5   Sally wanted to wear a .... to the party.

6   Sally went shopping at the .... that day.

7   The colour of her new dress was ....

On Sunday afternoon, she went to the party at Lucy's house in her new dress. Lucy saw Sally and Sally saw Lucy and they both started to laugh. 'We always wear jeans and T-shirts!' Sally said. 'But today we're both wearing dresses! Where did you buy yours?' 'At the market on Wednesday,' Lucy answered. 'And you?' 'At the market on Wednesday, like you!' laughed Sally. 'And I bought this for you there too.'

'Oh great! A CD! Thanks!' said Lucy.

8   The birthday party was on Sunday afternoon at

    ....

9   Both girls bought their dresses on .... from
    the market.

10 Sally gave Lucy .... for her birthday.

Blank Page

Part 6
– 5 questions –

Read the text. Choose the right words and write them on the lines.

Lions

Example   Lions are a kind of big cat. They live .... in ....

hot places. They are very strong animals and they can run

very quickly. They have very big teeth because they only

1   .... meat.

Lions like sitting on the ground or on rocks, and

2   .... in the sun. But because lions must

3   drink water .... day, you can sometimes

4   see .... next to a river. Smaller cats

5   .... not like being in water, but lions often

play or go swimming in it.

Example	at	in	on
1	eating	ate	eat
2	sleeps	sleeping	slept
3	every	any	another
4	it	him	them
5	do	have	are

Listening

Part 1
– 5 questions –

Listen and draw lines. There is one example.

Mary   Anna   Fred   Paul

Sally   Jim   Vicky

Part 2
– 5 questions –

Listen and write. There is one example.

Dance lessons for Daisy

	Where?	at ....school.............................
1	In which classroom?	....
2	On which day?	....
3	With which teacher?	Mrs ....
4	Take to first lesson:	....
5	Come home by:	....

Part 3

– 5 questions –

What did John do last week?

**Listen and draw a line from the day to the correct picture.
There is one example.**

Monday

Tuesday

Wednesday

Thursday

Friday

Saturday

Sunday

Part 4
– 5 questions –

Listen and tick (✔) the box. There is one example.

What's Tony doing?

A ☐   B ✔   C ☐

1   What did Jane buy yesterday?

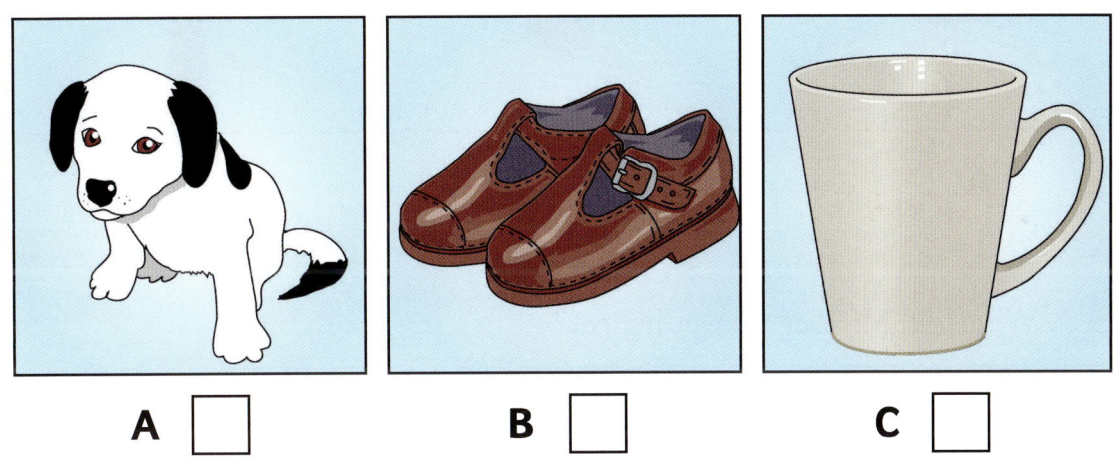

A ☐   B ☐   C ☐

2   What was Jack's dream about?

A ☐   B ☐   C ☐

3   Where's Peter's mouse?

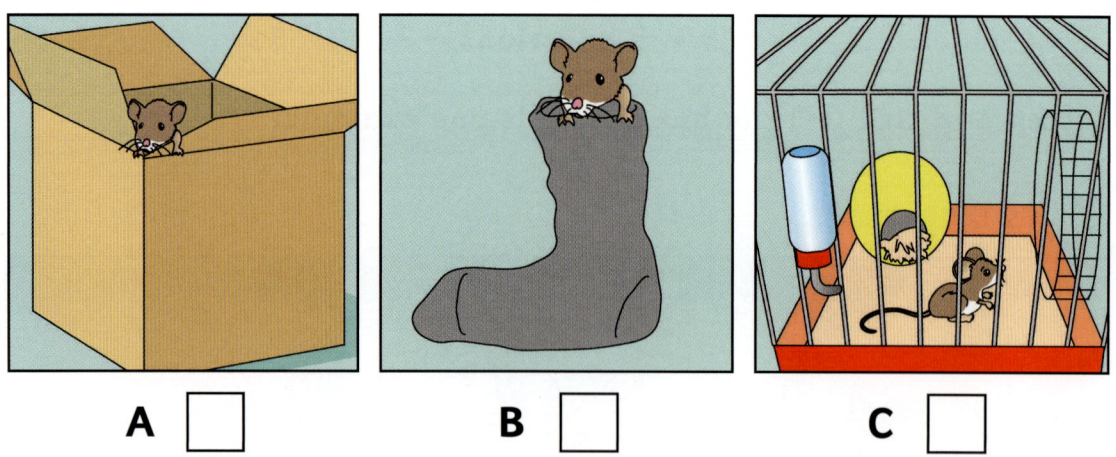

A   B   C

4   Which person is Kim?

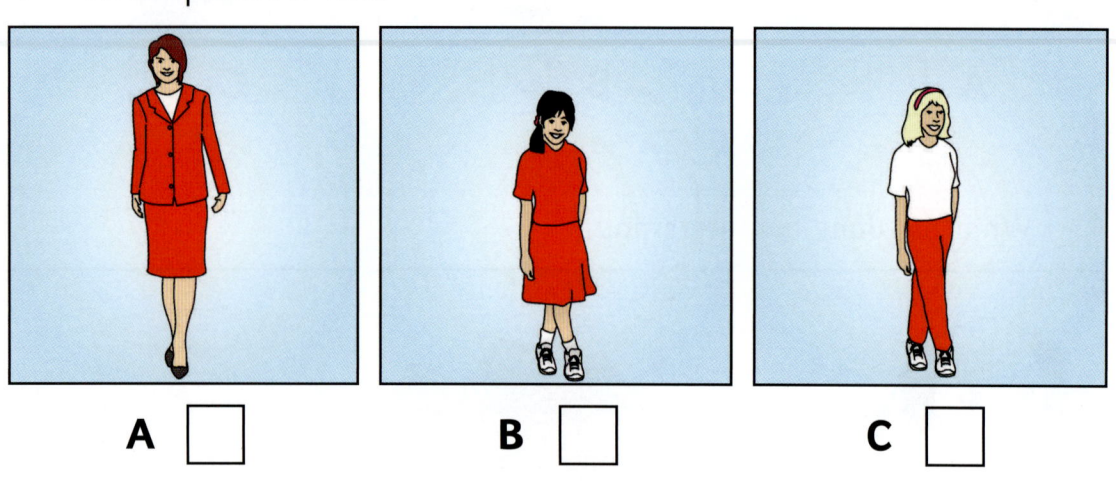

A   B   C

5   What did Mr Rice find in his car?

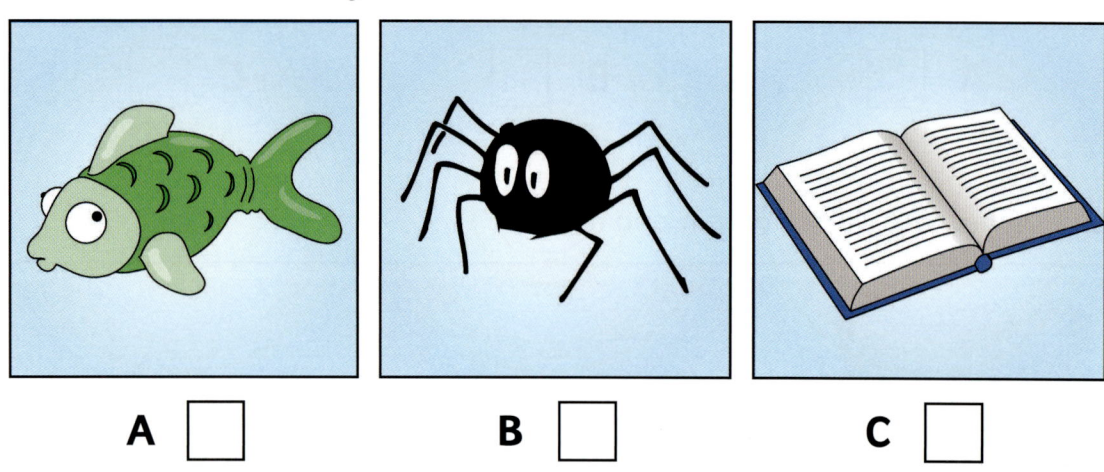

A   B   C

Part 5

– 5 questions –

Listen and colour and draw. There is one example.

Reading and Writing

Part 1
– 6 questions –

Look and read. Choose the correct words and write them on the lines. There is one example.

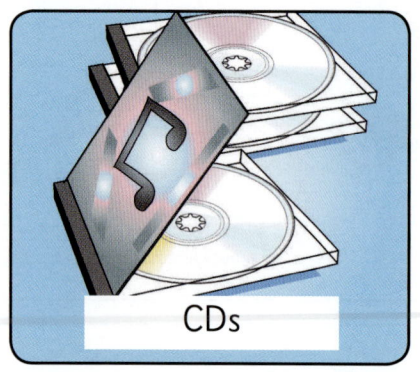

CDs

carrots

a snake

a bat

books

a panda

lemons

eggs

Example

We read these to learn things or to enjoy stories. ......*books*......

Questions

1   These come from chickens. We cook them and
     eat them.   ....

2   These often have music on them. We listen to
     them.   ....

3   This animal flies at night. Some people are
     afraid of it.   ....

4   People eat these vegetables. They are orange. ....

5   This animal is long and thin and it doesn't
     have any legs.   ....

6   You find this yellow fruit on trees.   ....

Part 2
– 6 questions –

Look and read. Write yes or no.

Examples

There are two comics on the bed.   *yes*
....

The child on the balcony is holding
a doll.   *no*
....

Questions

1   There is a rainbow behind the tree.   ....

2   The girl who has got long hair is
    sleeping.   ....

3   The smaller toy kangaroo is wearing
    a red scarf.   ....

4   The monkey is sitting between a
    plant and a bear.   ....

5   There is a black sweater under
    the chair.   ....

6   On the table there is a glass of
    fruit juice.   ....

Part 3

– 6 questions –

Read the text and choose the best answer.

Tom and his dad are on holiday in the forest.

Example

    Dad: Have you got your coat?

    Tom: Ⓐ   Yes, I have.
                B   Yes, I did.
                C   Yes, I can.

Questions

1   **Dad:**   Do you want to walk to the river?

     Tom: A   Good idea.
                  B   See you.
                  C   Me too.

2   **Tom:**   How about taking some sandwiches to the river?

    Dad: A   It was beautiful.
                  B   I enjoyed that.
                  C   OK, great!

3   **Tom:**   Look at those fish! They're very big!

    Dad: A   Yes, they are.
                  B   Yes, it is.
                  C   Yes, they do.

4   **Tom:**   Can I go fishing now, Dad?

    Dad: A   Every afternoon, Tom.
                  B   Last time, Tom.
                  C   After the picnic, Tom.

5   **Tom:**   This is a nice place, Dad. Let's have the sandwiches here.

    Dad: A   You weren't here.
                  B   OK, here they are.
                  C   He can eat it here.

6   **Tom:**   I love this place. I don't want to go home!

    Dad: A   Sorry, we have to go back tomorrow!
                  B   But we had to go before that.
                  C   Thanks, we can go then.

Part 4

– 7 questions –

Read the story. Choose a word from the box. Write the correct word next to numbers 1–6. There is one example.

Last Saturday, Paul went to his grandparents' house in the country. It was

a .... *sunny* .... day.

First, Paul had a (**1**) .... in his grandparents' swimming

pool. After that, he was very hungry. He ate the bread and sausages that

Grandma made for him, and then wanted more bread. Grandma looked in

the cupboard in the (**2**) .... but there wasn't any more.

She said, 'Could you go to the shop in the (**3**) .... ,

please, Paul?'

When Paul went into the street, Grandma's friend, Daisy, was there with

her horse. He stopped and (**4**) .... to her, and she said,

'Would you like to (**5**) .... my horse?' 'Yes, please!'

said Paul.

He went to the shop on the horse. He bought bread and two big

(**6**) ...., which he gave to the horse. Then he said

goodbye to Daisy and walked back to his grandparents' house.

Example

sunny	apples	carried
village	swim	ride
fields	kitchen	talked

(7) **Now choose the best name for the story.**

Tick one box.

Paul's day in the country ☐

Grandpa's horse ☐

Daisy's swimming pool ☐

Part 5
– 10 questions –

Look at the pictures and read the story. Write some words to complete the sentences about the story. You can use 1, 2 or 3 words. There are two examples.

<u>Peter's holiday</u>

Last holiday, Peter went to his cousin Sue's flat in the city.

On the first morning, the children played table tennis. Then Sue's mum said, 'Can you help me with lunch please?' Sue helped Mum with the food, but Peter did nothing.

Examples

Peter's cousin is called .... Sue ....

Sue lives .... in the city .... in a flat.

Questions

1   The children played .... on the first morning.

2   Only .... helped Mum.

After lunch, Sue washed the dirty bowls. Mum said, 'Peter, can you clean the table?' He said, 'No, I've got a headache.' He went to Sue's bedroom and played.

On the second day, Peter didn't get up. Mum said, 'Peter, Sue! Please come and make breakfast.' Peter said, 'I can't, I've got stomach-ache.' That evening, Mum said, 'Sue, would you like to go to the zoo in the morning?'

Both children said, 'Yes, please!' Mum said, 'But Peter, you can't go, you're not very well.' Peter said, 'I'm fine now.'

3   Sue washed some bowls after ....

4   Peter played in ....

5   Peter didn't help to make .... on the second day.

6   Mum wanted to take Sue to ....

➡️

On the third day, Peter got up before Sue and her mum and cleaned the house. When she saw this, Sue's mum was very surprised.

They all went to the zoo. Peter enjoyed looking at the lions, and Sue saw her favourite animals, which were the elephants. They went to a café for lunch and had a very nice day.

7 .... got up first on the third day.

8 Sue's mum was .... because Peter cleaned the house.

9 .... were Sue's favourite animals.

10 The family had lunch in a .... at the zoo.

Blank Page

Part 6

– 5 questions –

Read the text. Choose the right words and write them on the lines.

Whales

Example   Whales ....*live*......... in the sea.

1   There .... big whales and small whales.

2   The smallest whale is longer .... a man.

The biggest is the blue whale and it is very, very long. The blue

3   whale is the biggest and loudest animal ....

4   the world! Most whales sing songs to .... families.

5   All whales .... swim very fast. They move

quickly in the water and they like to jump out of the water.

Example	live	lives	living
1	was	is	are
2	or	than	but
3	in	of	on
4	them	their	they
5	can	be	have

Part 1
– 5 questions –

Listen and draw lines. There is one example.

John   Tony   Anna   Lucy

Peter   May   Bill

Part 2
– 5 questions –

Listen and write. There is one example.

People who come to our sports centre

Name:	Pat Jones	
Which sport?	tennis	
1	Comes here by:	
2	When?	in the
3	Who with?	his
4	Doesn't like:	
5	How old?	

Part 3
– 5 questions –

What did Ben do last week?

Listen and draw a line from the day to the correct picture.

There is one example.

Monday

Tuesday

Wednesday

Thursday

Friday

Saturday

Sunday

Part 4

– 5 questions –

Listen and tick (✔) the box. There is one example.

What's Mary doing?

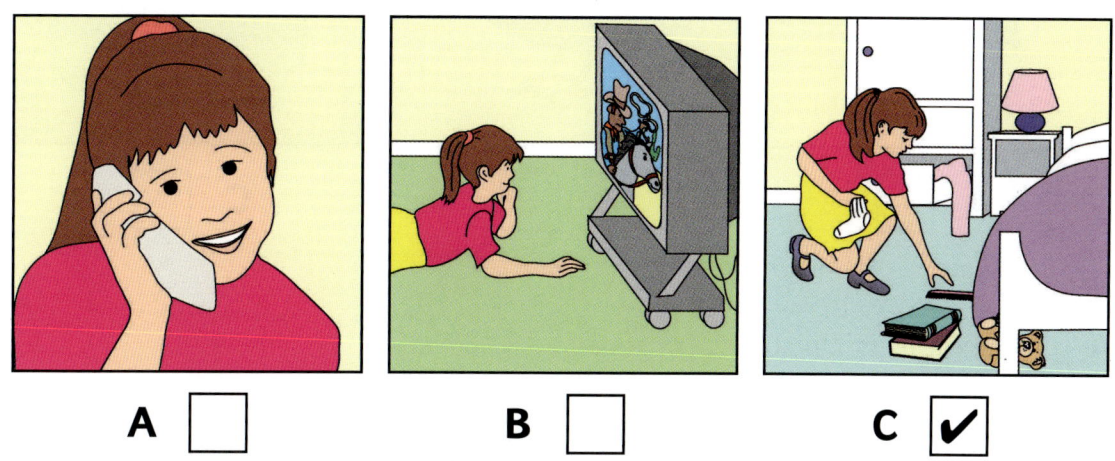

A ☐　　　B ☐　　　C ✔

1　Where did Alex walk to today?

A ☐　　　B ☐　　　C ☐

2　What has Jack got for lunch today?

A ☐　　　B ☐　　　C ☐

3   What kind of pet does Fred have?

A ☐   B ☐   C ☐

4   Which girl is Daisy?

A ☐   B ☐   C ☐

5   What's the weather like at Jane's house today?

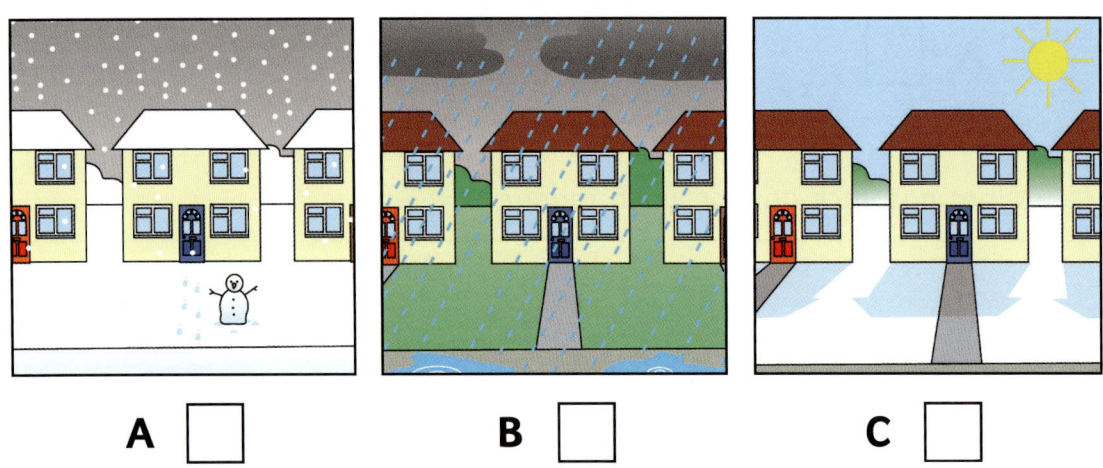

A ☐   B ☐   C ☐

Part 5

– 5 questions –

Listen and colour and draw. There is one example.

Reading and Writing

Part 1

– 6 questions –

Look and read. Choose the correct words and write them on the lines. There is one example.

forests

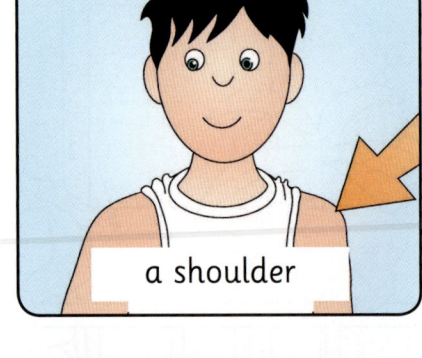

a shoulder

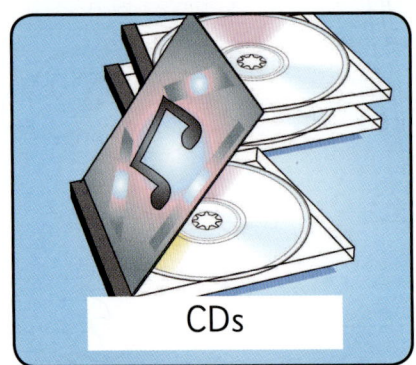

CDs

a beard

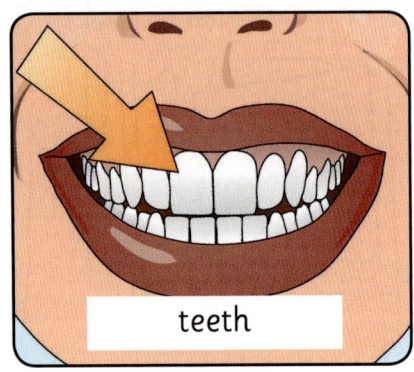

teeth

DVDs

comics

plants

Example

This is hair on a man's face.   .... *a beard* ....

Questions

1   Children like to read these. They have
    pictures in them.   ....

2   These are in your mouth and they are white.   ....

3   Most of these have leaves on them and
    some have flowers.   ....

4   These are films that you can watch on
    your television.   ....

5   This is part of your body. It is at the top
    of your arm.   ....

6   These are places that have a lot of trees.   ....

Part 2
– 6 questions –

Look and read. Write yes or no.

Examples

There are six children at the party.   ....yes...............

It's raining outside.   ....no...............

Questions

1   All the children are wearing hats,
    which are orange.   ....

2   The girl who has got straight blonde
    hair is eating a sandwich.   ....

3   The clown is coming downstairs to
    the dining room.   ....

4   The man is carrying a bowl of fruit
    in his hands.   ....

5   There is a bottle of lemonade on
    the floor.   ....

6   The woman is drawing a picture of
    the children.   ....

Part 3
– 6 questions –

Read the text and choose the best answer.

Daisy and her grandmother are talking about Daisy's new school.

Example

Daisy:	Hello, Grandmother. How are you?

Grandmother:	A	Thank you, Daisy.
	B	Here you are, Daisy.
	Ⓒ	Hello, Daisy. I'm very well.

Questions

1	**Grandmother:**	Did you enjoy your first day at school, Daisy?

Daisy:	A	Yes, I enjoy it.
	B	Yes, it was very good.
	C	Yes, I went to school today.

2   **Grandmother:**   How many children are there in your class?

     Daisy: A   The classroom is very big.
                   B   There are eight classes in the school.
                   C   There are 10 girls and 12 boys.

3   **Grandmother:**   Did you walk to school?

     Daisy: A   No, I rode my bike.
                   B   No, I wasn't there.
                   C   No, I didn't have one.

4   **Grandmother:**   What's your teacher's name?

     Daisy: A   The teacher knew my name.
                   B   Her name's Mrs Page.
                   C   Mrs Brown took me to school.

5   **Grandmother:**   Which sports do you play at school?

     Daisy: A   I like playing on the computer.
                   B   We can play sports at school.
                   C   Hockey and basketball.

6   **Daisy:**   I have to do my homework now, Grandmother.

     Grandmother: A   OK. Goodbye, Daisy.
                         B   Yes, I do, Daisy.
                         C   I'd love to, Daisy.

Part 4

– 7 questions –

Read the story. Choose a word from the box. Write the correct word next to numbers 1–6. There is one example.

Yesterday, John and Jane and their mum and dad had breakfast in the

.........garden............ . Their pet rabbit was with them. His name is Skip.

It was a hot, (**1**)......................... morning and Skip was thirsty. He

saw Dad's (**2**)......................... of coffee and he drank some coffee

from it. John ran to stop the rabbit and he (**3**)......................... 'No,

don't drink that, Skip!'

In the afternoon, Skip didn't look well. 'Let's take him to the animal

hospital,' said Jane. Dad took them in the car. A (**4**).........................

looked at the rabbit. 'He's got stomach-ache. Coffee is very bad for rabbits,'

she told them. 'He needs to drink lots of water now, and he can eat

(**5**)......................... too.'

Skip drank some water, and in the evening he started to

(**6**)......................... again. The children were very happy.

Example

garden

cup

hungry

shouted

nurse

sunny

danced

hop

carrots

(7) Now choose the best name for the story.

Tick one box.

John's stomach-ache ☐

Skip isn't well ☐

Jane goes to a café ☐

Part 5
– 10 questions –

Look at the pictures and read the story. Write some words to complete the sentences about the story. You can use 1, 2 or 3 words. There are two examples.

A day at the zoo with Uncle Fred

My name is Paul. Last Sunday Uncle Fred took my sister Sally and me to the zoo. It was a cold, windy day and we had to wear hats and scarves. We went on the train and I sat next to the window. We went to see the panda first, then we looked at the elephants. They were very big and very strong.

Examples

Paul's sister is called ....*Sally*...................... .

The weather was ....*cold and windy*........... on the day that Paul, Sally and Uncle Fred went to the zoo.

Questions

1   They went to the zoo by ....

2   The first animal that they saw at the zoo was the

     ....

After lunch, Sally chose to see the monkeys. Giraffes are her favourite animals but there weren't any at the zoo. I wanted to take a photo of Sally with the monkeys. She took off her scarf and put it on a wall. One of the monkeys picked up her scarf and put it on. I took a photo of the monkey because it looked funny.

3   .... wanted to see the monkeys after lunch.

4   There weren't any .... at the zoo.

5   A monkey wore Sally's ....

6   The monkey looked funny and Paul .... of it.

Then I wanted to see the dolphins because they're my favourite animals.

When Uncle Fred took a photo of me next to the pool, a dolphin came out of the water and hit a ball with its nose. 'Oh no!' I laughed. 'Now all my clothes are wet!' Uncle Fred laughed and said, 'Here, Paul, put my coat on.' 'Thank you,' I said. Then Uncle Fred said, 'Now let's go home,' and we did.

7   The animals that Paul likes best are ....

8   The dolphin's nose hit a ....

9   Paul's clothes were .... because the dolphin came out of the water near him.

10   Uncle Fred gave Paul his .... and then they went home.

Blank Page

Part 6
– 5 questions –

Read the text. Choose the right words and write them on the lines.

Libraries

Example

A library is a place that .... **has** .... books for people to read.

A lot of schools have libraries and you can find a library in most cities and in some smaller towns. Today most libraries

1 .... not only have books, newspapers and magazines. They sometimes have computers and DVDs too.

2 You can read the books in the library .... you can choose your books there, and then take

3 .... home to read.

In some parts of the world the library is in a kind

4 .... bus, which goes to small villages to

5 take books to people .... cannot go to the

library in the town.

Example	had	has	having
1	do	have	are
2	than	because	or
3	them	they	it
4	from	of	for
5	what	who	whose

Blank Page

Speaking

Find the differences

Picture Story

Odd-one-out

Blank Page

Find the differences

Picture Story

Odd-one-out

Blank Page

Speaking

Picture Story

Odd-one-out